Mindful Mosaic

Abstract Doodles to Color

by JoAnne Lehman

Zwerg Acres Productions

Madison, Wisconsin

2015

Published in the United States by Zwerg Acres Productions, Madison, Wisconsin
Printed by CreateSpace, an Amazon.com company

ISBN-13: 978-0692600542 (Zwerg Acres Productions)
ISBN-10: 069260054X

Printed in the United States of America
First Edition

Welcome to Mindful Mosaic...

Is that a shell? A pile of rocks? Waves, leaves, clouds? A stained glass window? Or just an inviting group of lines and shapes? And what do you want to do with it? It's all up to you, and it doesn't matter what you decide. This coloring book is a no-pressure invitation — to play, explore, focus, dream, or rest.

These abstract, mosaic-style doodles can stimulate your imagination, free you from constraints, and pull you into a whimsical world of color. Color the shapes, color the spaces between the shapes, or color both. Emphasize patterns or fill spaces randomly. Use ninety-six colors or six, or just one! Get out a fine-tip pen and add to the designs — draw in borders, or shapes within or around the given shapes. There are even some blank pages at the end to fill with your own completely original doodles.

You can also cut the pages out of the book — we've put in extra inside margin width for that purpose — and turn them any way you choose, because there's no definite up, down, right or left to the designs. Frame your finished work — or use it for wrapping paper, or cut it up into bookmarks and laminate them! It's all up to you.

"Mindfulness." Being "in the moment." Calming unhelpful thought patterns. Engaging in "creative flow." Loosening the hold of negative thought loops. Such terminology is emerging in the field of mental health to describe processes of attaining and maintaining good mental and emotional hygiene — of shifting from a stress-driven body/mind state to a "resting or repairing" body/mind state. Many adults are rediscovering coloring — an activity that until recently was thought of as child's play — as one very practical way to accomplish such a shift.

When you look at patterns of freeform black lines and spaces on a white page, the impulse to add color can be irresistible! Whether you sink into these drawings for hours or just for a few minutes, the stresses of life (and of your busy brain) can fade away as you decide which color to reach for next.

Because the images are non-representational, you don't need to worry about making them "look like something." You can decide what these drawings should look like, or refrain from consciously deciding anything at all — just start coloring. When you have finished a piece, it will look just the way it needs to look.

Here's pressure-free creativity. A time-out for your busy or worried mind. A way to shift from stress to serenity.

— JoAnne Lehman, December 2015

with huge thanks to design consultant,
mental health consultant, &
incredible life partner M.K.

Ready to shift from stress to rest and repair?

Grab some crayons, colored pencils, pens, markers, or paints — anything at all! (If you choose markers or paints, you might want to slide a piece of scrap paper underneath your page in case of bleed-through). Go for it. It's all up to you.

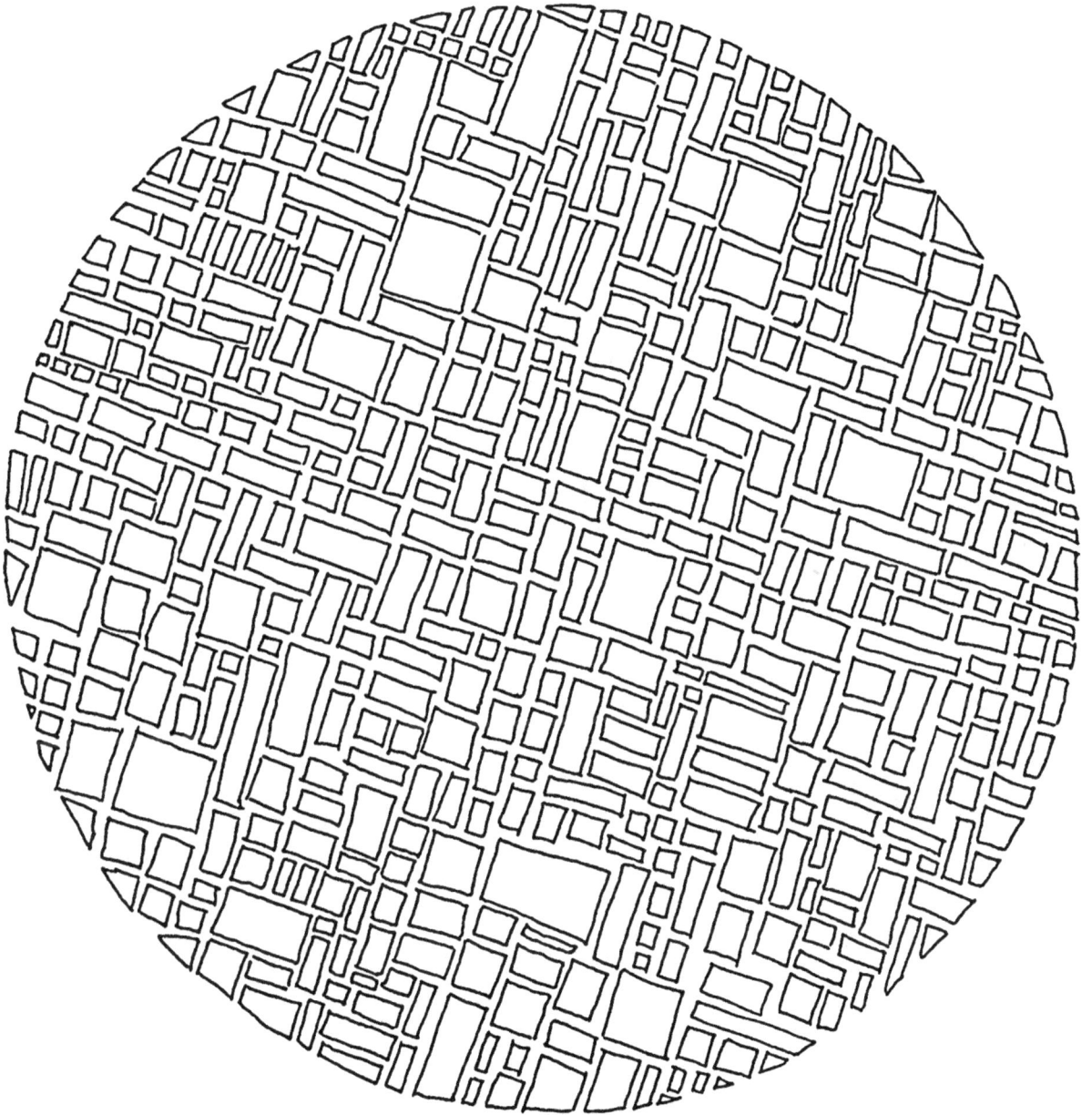

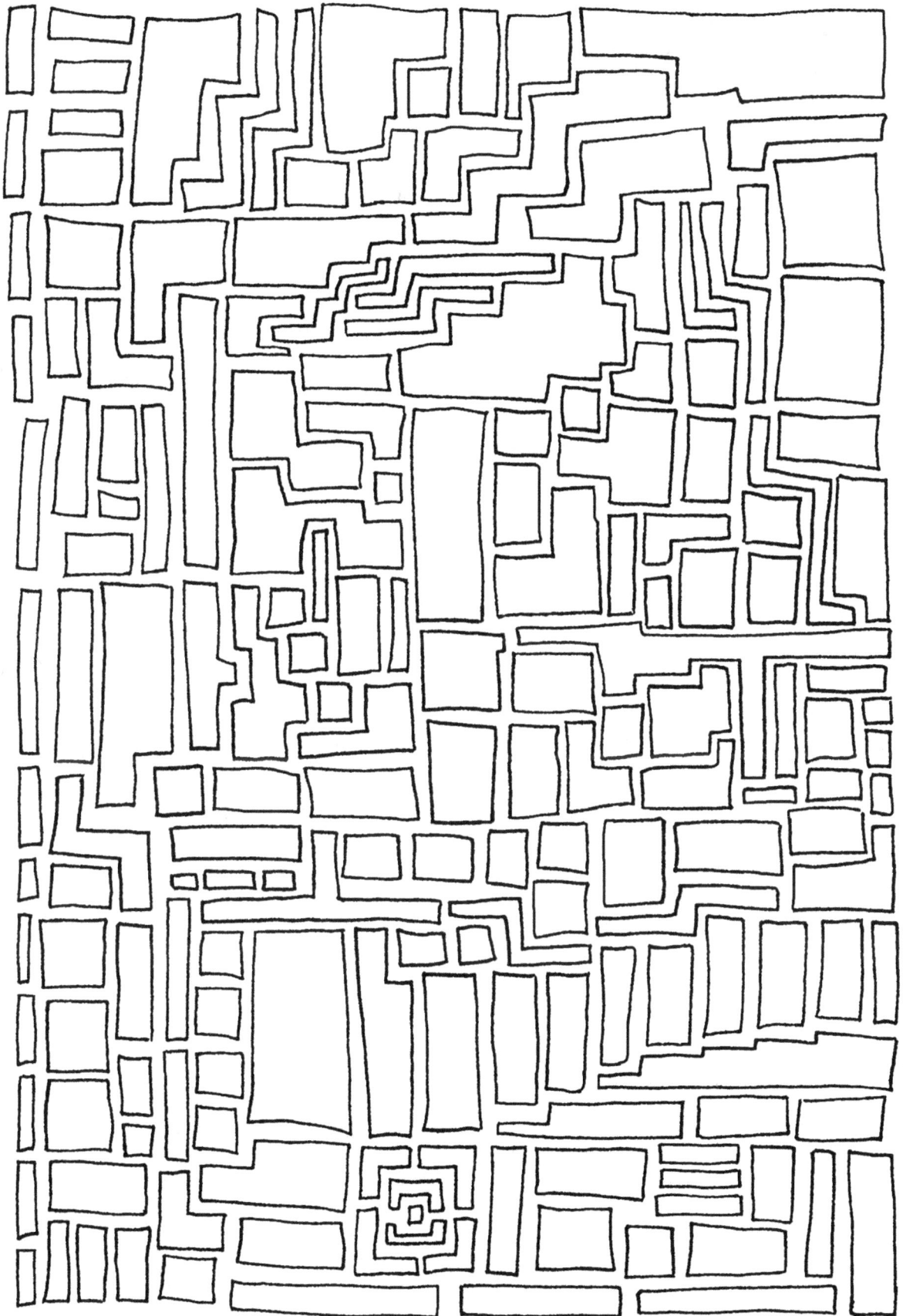

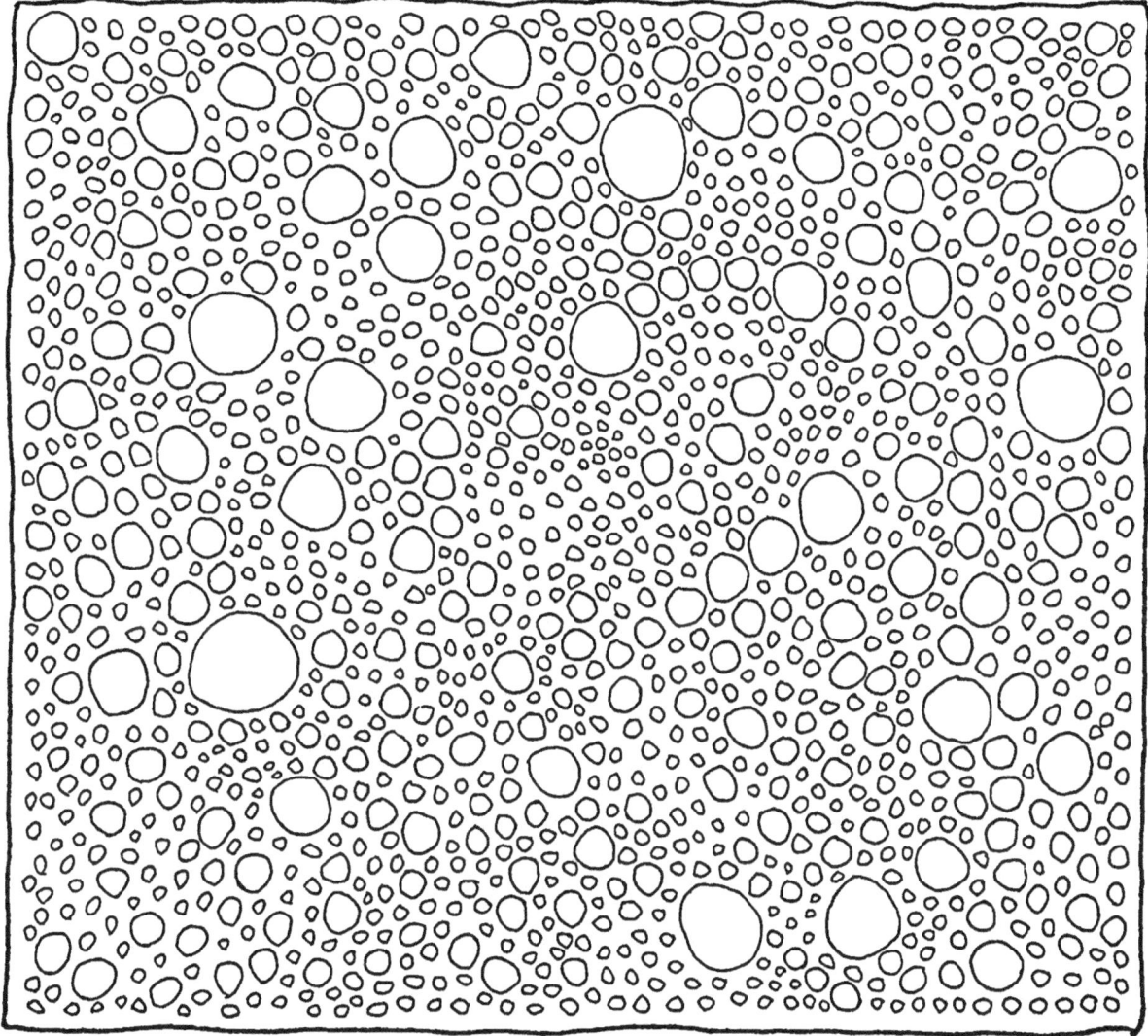

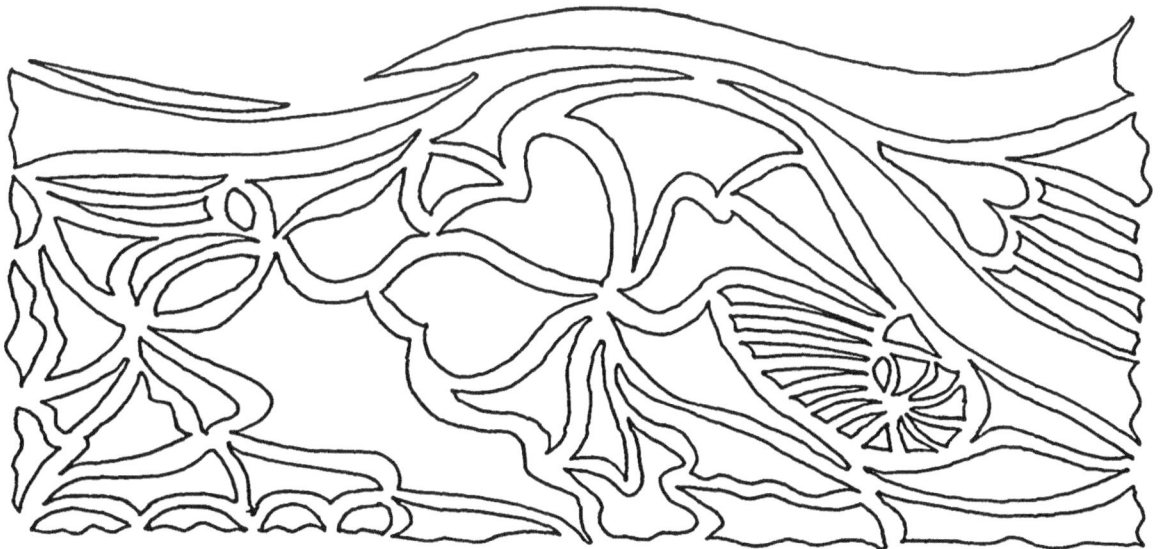

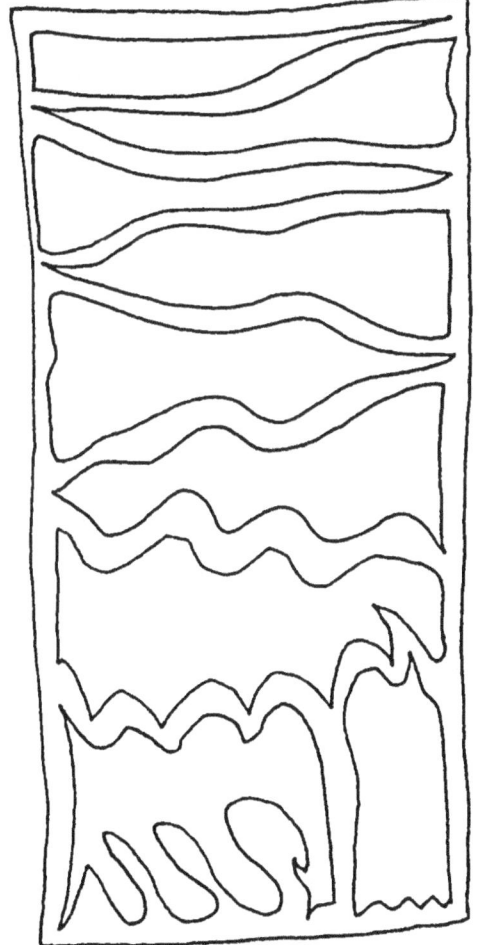